Welcome to She's Inspired Paper & Co.

Our designs are made to inspire women to leave their mark on not just these pages, but also on the world.

In this notebook, you'll find a place to record ideas, dream big dreams, plan new paths, start a journaling practice, or write whatever serves your greater purpose.

Above all, we are about women uplifting other women.

So, don't keep this to yourself:
Get a notebook for a woman who inspires you!

Follow us at @sheisinspiredco on Instagram

Made in the USA
Monee, IL
26 February 2022

91877149R00072